LOCAL Church GIRL

Beloved & Called

Written by

Nicole DeBehnke

ISBN: 9798269341859

Dedication

To my precious children, Noah, Caylee, and Jack. I chose to live my life for God before you, replicating His plans and not my own or the world's. I love everything about you guys, you are one of the best honors I have to love, lead, and champion in life. I'm always here for you, darlings.

To the precious women who pick up this study I pray that this ignites restoration, love, and a deep value for the local body of Christ. May the words in these pages bless you and help you in all that you do as a believer. May we be planted together in His Church, fully effective, lacking no good thing.

Acknowledgments

Thank you to my Heavenly Father. You've found and restored me through your precious Son, Jesus, my Savior. Thank you for continuing to reveal yourself to me through your Holy Word. I'll wait here patiently, enjoying the precious family you've gifted me while serving you faithfully, until I get to meet you face to face. How I long to hear you say, "Well done, Nicole."

A special thank you to my seen and unseen friends, sisters, and family. I love you each and am so thankful that God brought you into my life. Thank you for your prayers, sweet encouragement, understanding hearts, and deep support. I'm cheering you on as you each continue to pursue God's plan for your life and expand God's footprint wherever you go!

And last but certainly not least, the love of my life, my best friend, and forever pick-me-up, Chris. Thank you for everything you have done and continue to do for me and our family. Your love, support, and partnership are priceless to me. You constantly inspire me to draw closer to God and be all He has called and freed me to be. Thank you for pushing me, leading me, fighting for me, protecting me, and loving me deeply. I am grateful to build a life with you this side of heaven.

Table of Contents

Introduction

I was talking with a new friend who was sharing her faith with me and how she was standing for her family's salvation. I was listening to her pour her heart out, and then I asked, "What church do you go to?" She quickly replied, "Oh, I don't go to church, I don't need to go to be close to God." She didn't know, but my heart sank silently. I was so sad to hear her say that so confidently, as if to defend her stance.

After that talk, I was bothered by what she said and began to recall many other women in my life who believe in Jesus but don't have a church or don't attend regularly; in fact, some are resistant to going. I began replaying that sentence I'd heard consistently over the years, and again my heart sank even deeper. Why, Lord, why are so many people saying this so freely and confidently as if to defend their reason for not being planted in a local church body? What is it that is stopping them? Is it hurt, shame, pride, fear, myths about church... I don't know, Lord, but I'm sad and bothered by this.

After this, I was stirred to write something and then shared it on social media. I realized I was a Local Church Girl through and through and that I deeply wanted others to see the value of the local church body and find their place within it. The Lord was awakening a movement in me that I had yet to discover. The more I sat with Him about this idea, the more He expanded my vision and unpacked it as I walked out the steps He laid before me. Getting His girls excited and proud about being planted in the local body and part of the cause of Christ instead of silently trying to live out their faith in hurt, shame, pride, fear, or misunderstanding. I want to see 2 Peter 1 come alive in all believers' lives, where more and more of them are not ineffective in the gospel but the exact opposite, never failing in it!

Many women identify as Christian, yet many of them are disconnected and not planted in a local church body, bearing fruit, serving others, and benefiting from the community of Christ. What do you think? Maybe it's the real hypocrisy they have unfortunately seen or experienced. Maybe it's church hurt or a false belief about not needing the local body and its role in our lives. Whatever it is, I believe God wants to reveal to us how we can help fill the local Church with God's precious and beloved people. Whether you have just given your life to Christ, you've been a believer for years, or are a minister of the gospel, God has so much in store for you and the influence you have in building the local presence of the church. I'm excited to encourage and stir you on as God brings you awareness, healing, and hope along the way. ***My goal is to recapture the women on the fringe and gather them into the house so together we can expand the footprint of God's hope for the world through Jesus Christ in our local churches across the globe.***

Posted July 16, 2025

I'm a local church girl.
Beloved and called.
Formed and found.
Forgiven and encouraged.

God has changed my life.
And so has His precious Church.

I don't just have a relationship with God through Christ...
I have a relationship with His beloved people through Christ.

I am affirmed.
Loved.
Full of purpose.

And still ...I struggle.
No one is perfect except Jesus.
But we are being perfected in Him.

So I say this with love:
Show up.
Don't quit the church because a few people are still being
sanctified.
Keep going.

If it's possible on your part, pursue peace with everyone.

Be a forgiver.

Be sober-minded.

And never forget how much YOU'VE been redeemed.

Cheering you on.

Get planted and bear fruit.

Let's value the local church and make its footprint larger together in Christ. Thank you for joining me on this journey as we discover together how we can encourage one another in Christ. As Scripture says, not to forsake the assembling together of the saints. If you don't know yet, the word "saints" is another word for "followers of Jesus or believers." We don't want to neglect gathering with other believers. This new life God offers us through Christ happens best in the context of relationships, not alone.

We don't get saved to live isolated and shy about share our faith; actually, it's the complete opposite. We get saved and then, little by little, God transforms us into the image of Christ through the power and leading of the Holy Spirit at work in our lives. This is true and powerful for both extroverts and introverts. That same Spirit leads and guides us into the things of God through truth. As you will discover later in this study, we are all bound together through the power of the Holy Spirit to form the body of Christ, the Church.

Do you long to see your family, friends, and neighbors saved? Do you desire to sit, pray, worship, and serve alongside them? I believe you do, I believe you want to be bold in your faith and hope in Christ. I, for one, am sick of seeing people I know and love live without the hope I have in Christ.

I believe that is why you have picked up this study; deep down, you want to bring others into a relationship with Christ. You want to see the church grow and communities changed; you believe in the power of the body of Christ, even if you don't know all the blessings it consists of yet.

So, even though we don't need the church to be saved, we do need the community, support, and the accountability it offers to help us stand and grow in the things of God. Other people in our lives reveal and flesh out our sinful nature, and to become more like Christ, we all need one another, especially believers. Let's step back and gain a clearer picture of the local church and our lives. The local church influences and impacts communities just like you influence and impact people.

Therefore, brothers, since we have confidence to enter the holy places by the blood of Jesus, by the new and living way that He opened for us through the curtain, that is, through His flesh, and since we have a great priest over the house of God, let us draw near with a true heart in full assurance of faith, with our hearts sprinkled clean from an evil conscience and our bodies washed with pure water. Let us hold fast the confession of our hope without wavering, for he who promised is faithful. **And let us consider how to stir up one another to love and good works, not neglecting to meet together, as is the habit of some, but encouraging one another, and all the more as you see the day drawing near.**

Hebrews 10:19-25

HOW IT ALL BEGAN
WEEK 1

HOW IT ALL BEGAN
Week 1

Saved By Grace.

We are going to begin this study one step at a time, going from glory to glory. Which simply means God transforms us from one level of His glory to the next, becoming more and more like Christ. As it happens, all of us have the same first step, and that is salvation. Whether it was just recently or years ago, we had a moment with the Lord where He revealed Himself to us and offered salvation through His precious Son, Jesus Christ.

Where were you when this special moment took place?

Do you remember the details leading up to it and how you knew in your heart that you needed and wanted Jesus to be your Lord and Savior?

I remember mine and love sharing the story with others. I was fourteen and had grown up in and out of church, finding myself back in Florida with no friends after spending the last semester of eighth grade as an exchange student in Finland. Most of my friends had forgotten about me and were not going to the same high school as I was, so I was desperate for friends. When I got back from Finland, my parents took us to my aunt's house, where they were having a water baptism for my cousins. After the baptism, my cousin invited me to church with him, and, of course, I said yes. That night, I walked in, and honestly, I was instantly embarrassed to be there because a couple of days prior, at the water baptism, I had flipped off the youth leader teaching the message, —my now husband, Chris. I tried to hide in the back of the room, waiting for the night to begin so it could be over and I could leave.

But something happened during that service, and I didn't know it then, but it was the work of the Holy Spirit. God was illuminating Himself to me in a way I had never heard before, even though I had grown up in and out of the church. There was nothing fancy about the night; in fact, it was a small room with a pixelated projector, still images and no live music. Instead, a living God was in the room, making Himself known to the people who showed up.

By the end of the service, they asked if anyone in the room wanted to give their life to Christ. My heart had been stirring the whole service, and all the embarrassment that I walked in with was no match for the love God was revealing to me in His precious Son, Jesus. I quickly raised my hand and made eye contact with the youth pastor, and the rest is HIS-story in me. I've never been the same and never walked alone since that day. I have still had struggles and hard things happen to me, but the difference is I've never walked alone since.

I share this precious moment of mine with you to remind you that someone played a part in your salvation. For me, it was a culmination of people who shared Jesus with me throughout my childhood, and my bold cousin who invited me to church that night. He didn't need to, and honestly, he could have just told me about Jesus, as he had several times, and been like, 'Okay, I tried; she's not coming... I did my best.' But he didn't stop sowing seeds in my heart about Jesus, and in that youth room, God continued using other people to water those seeds in my heart until God brought the increase, which was the gift of salvation.

My story doesn't end there. I didn't get saved and then stop going to church —actually, the opposite happened. I jumped into all that God had for me. I wanted to be in His house all the time. I wanted to serve the God who formed, found, and called me, and since then, I have faithfully been in the house of God, the same church where I was saved. Yes, there have been painful moments with others. I have had to deal with my own selfishness and pride, even shame that has tried to take me out, leading me with lies that I don't belong or I can't get too close to others because I might get hurt again and again and again. While all of that and more is true and does happen, it's not because of God but because everyone in the church, even the pastors, are still being sanctified through the Word of God. We will still miss it this side of heaven. But this is what God does: He redeems and restores, giving us a new life in Him. He chooses to use the weak and make them strong in Him, a place where His glory shines and draws others to Himself. I'm thirty-six now, and this new life is better than anything I could have ever imagined. I am married to my best friend, we have three precious children, and God continues to surround me with goodness, treasured friends, and family to do life with. I am so thankful for God's body of believers, so many of them have impacted my life for the better, helping and encouraging me to walk out God's plan for my life.

So, no, the church is not perfect, but the Savior of the Church is, and He has actually given us all we need to heal and live in peace with one another. Not because of what they do, but because of what He can do in us to help us overcome the very real hurt and pain of relationships. One of those ways is remembering our salvation first. Remembering that we have each fallen short of perfection and that, in fact, we have earned the penalty of sin, eternal separation from God. But God, in His generous compassion, made a way for us to be fully saved and redeemed through the perfect and precious sacrifice of Jesus Christ. Leading up to our salvation through Jesus was long-suffering, patience, and a hope that one day we would turn to the knowledge of Christ and surrender fully.

Do you remember when you weren't so lovely, when you needed long-suffering, when you needed patience, and so much more? When we remember that we weren't and aren't perfect, it's so much easier to look at others with grace and extend that same grace that was lavished over us. Remember, we are saved by grace, the gift of God, not by our effort or how much we serve, not how much we give or suffer; all that matters is what God did for us through His Son Jesus and our personal response to the gift of salvation.

Something my husband and I do that helps us operate in grace and understanding toward one another is when one person messes up, we don't act like they never did anything or try to suffer in silence. No, we go to the person and tell them in love with tact, "Hey when you did that it hurt my feelings" or "When you said that I feel like you don't see what I do" and so on. When we respond in love and honesty, we keep the door open to grace that says, "We've got the rest of our marriage to get it right". We don't dig our feet into the sand and say, "You better straighten up and get it right, cause if you miss it again, game over". No, godly love cannot flourish like that and thank God He never played that hand even though He's the only one who could. Even in the Old Testament, before the cross, we see God persistently giving humanity the opportunity to turn back to Him.

Another way to look at this is to understand the distinction between salvation and sanctification. When we get saved, we are saved and redeemed from the penalty of sin once and for all. We only need to be saved one time. Simultaneously, the process of sanctification begins to take place in our lives. We don't sanctify ourselves; rather, God sanctifies us through the Holy Scriptures, the Holy Spirit, and our obedience. This process is also known as "a setting apart" for something special or to make holy.

Sanctification is progressive because it is a daily practice of laying one's flesh down and operating in the new created Spirit we were given when we accept Christ as our Lord and Savior. When we get saved, we don't just become perfect and stop sinning. Actually, we still have a sin nature on earth, and that sin nature needs to be rejected daily; otherwise, we will not be transformed into the image of Christ. Little by little, we are being set apart to be used by God as image bearers of Christ.

Look at what Jesus says to the disciples as they are supposed to be keeping watch for Him before He is taken away after being betrayed by Judas.

'Watch and pray that you may not enter into temptation. The Spirit indeed is willing, but the flesh is weak." 'Matthew 26:41

He says the Spirit is willing, but the flesh is weak. That confirms the conflict of our sin nature and our new nature at war daily in all believers, no matter how close you are to Jesus. This conflict does not go away when you get saved; it is revealed through living in proximity to Jesus. The closer we grow towards Christ, the more our sin nature is revealed, and God helps us overcome that sin nature through the wonderful help of the Holy Spirit and not through condemnation. It's the love of God that draws sinners to repentance.

Paul says it like this. 'But I say, walk by the spirit, and you will not gratify the desires of the flesh. For the desires of the flesh are against the spirit, and the desires of the spirit are against the flesh, for these are opposed to each other, to keep you from doing the things you want to do. 'Galatians 5:16-17

As I shared when I got saved, I wanted to be at the church whenever I could, and I literally did not want to miss a thing. I started attending youth group, then moved on to Wednesday nights, Sunday mornings, serve days, and eventually served at the church in various capacities. The community of other believers trusting God with their lives influenced me to seek God for my own life. I was surrounded by breakthroughs, life changes, testimonies, and people walking in God's divine favor and possibility. The powerful part was that I wasn't met with condemnation in our church; I was met by God's love in His people, which drew me to change.

When I was younger, I struggled with lying. Before I was saved, I even put on a tough persona at school so no one would mess with me.

But as I attended church and heard the Word of God, I began to change and desired to be trustworthy. I started to see my character as something meaningful and worshipful to God rather than "rules." I began seeking God for my own breakthrough, and as I learned more about Him and experienced His goodness, I wanted to worship Him even more. That same Spirit that revealed Christ to me in that youth room was the same Spirit revealing transformation to me through others, not all at once, but step by step, with the whole intent to transform me into the image of Christ.

What could you be wrestling with? I can tell you that I still wrestle with sin and the first response of my flesh, especially in situations that resemble pain or when I am tired, not feeling well, or overwhelmed. But God is not looking for perfection in me; He is looking for willingness and humility. I love what my husband says, "I've never made my best decisions after midnight." I have ungodly thoughts that pop into my head and try to distort the truth, or even thoughts that try to prompt desires for sin. The more I seek God and His will, the more I find freedom from my will, all through the gift of grace. All we can offer God is our trust and obedience, nothing more and nothing less.

If you get a chance, read Romans chapter 7, where Paul describes this tension in more detail. The law, which is known as the 10 commandments, reveals the sin nature already within us because of the fall and without Jesus, we have to earn our salvation through living perfectly, which we cannot do. That is why God appointed priests in the Old Testament to transfer our sin to a sacrificial animal to temporarily cover us for a year. But Jesus paid this price for all of humanity through His sacrifice, and when we accept this eternal non-temporary gift, we are born again into Christ. When we are born again, we are given a new created Spirit in which the Holy Spirit resides until we reach heaven. The Spirit and the flesh are at odds, and the only way to live by the Spirit is to die to the flesh daily. Daily in the word, in His presence, in prayer and in yielding to His ways, not ours or the ways of the world.

Jesus is our new eternal High priest and what He did is not temporary but eternal. The Word says that believers can confidently draw near to the throne of Grace to receive mercy and grace to help us when we are struggling. His grace is not temporary or something we can earn and get. No, it is freely given to us, something we cannot trade effort for. It is unmerited and truly a gift. Not only are we clothed with righteousness because of

Jesus, but we receive mercy because we are not perfect and grace to help us overcome. But we need to go to Him to receive this mercy and grace; otherwise condemnation and guilt will trap us into earning righteousness through works, and if we're not careful, we will convince others to earn it too.

Grace helps us put things in the right perspective and reminds us that we are waging war against spiritual principalities rather than people. If we are not careful, our flesh can puff us up in pride, and we will begin to war against people instead of the real battle at hand.

'For we do not wrestle against flesh and blood, but against the rulers, against the authorities, against the cosmic powers over this present darkness, against the spiritual forces of evil in the heavenly places. 'Ephesians 6:12

Let's take a moment in this next section called "Time to Reflect and Reject." Over the next six weeks, you'll use these pages and questions to help you process what the Holy Spirit is revealing to you through each chapter. Remember, this reflection is meant to be personal. We're not focusing on discerning others' fruits, but rather on our own. It's easy to think we know what others need to change, but this time, let's look inward and allow the Holy Spirit to reveal areas where He's inviting us to grow.

In Matthew 7:3-5, Jesus reminds us to take the log out of our own eye before looking to others to see a speck in their eye. You got this!

"Let us test and examine our ways, and return to the Lord!"
Lamentations 3:40

"Search me, O God, and know my heart! Try me and know my thoughts! And see if there be any grievous way in me, and lead me in the way everlasting!"
Psalm 139:23–24

TIME TO REFLECT AND REJECT

What is your salvation story and who do you think played a part in praying for you or sowing seeds of Jesus in your life?

_____

_____

_____

_____

_____

_____

Even though you are saved, do you see that conflict of your flesh and Spirit like Paul talks about?

_____

_____

_____

_____

_____

_____

How do you feel about sanctification and is it something you are actively doing daily? If not, how could you start incorporating it into your daily life?

_____

_____

_____

_____

_____

_____

How do you think remembering your salvation journey can help you look at others through the lens of grace?

_____

_____

_____

_____

_____

_____

Remember the body of Christ is not perfect, but the Savior of the Church is, and He has done everything for us to live from glory to glory individually and together, all for God's glory and not our own. The Local Church is a beautiful community of people who are trying their best to surrender and be sanctified, including you and me.

A SOBER MIND
WEEK 2

A SOBER MIND
Week 2

Being sober-minded helps you live in peace and stay faithfully planted in the Church.

'Be sober-minded; be watchful. Your adversary the devil prowls around like a roaring lion, seeking someone to devour. '
1 Peter 5:8

Have you ever wondered what it means to be sober-minded or to have sober judgment? Well, I have, and let me tell you, it's not what I thought it was, but I'm glad the Lord revealed it to me. The biblical definition of a sober mind is a state of clarity and awareness found in self-control, a fruit of the Spirit.

So, to be sober-minded is to have self-control over one's emotions and feelings. It is to keep clarity and sound judgment in moments when life becomes chaotic, messy, or overwhelming. Think of the natural definition of sober vs. intoxication. If we are intoxicated with alcohol, we lack self-control though some would foolishly argue. Excessive alcohol loosens us up and relaxes us so we're less vigilant and aware. It is like hitting the off button and if we drink too much then we risk embarrassment and regret because of too much comfort and a lack of self-control. It takes time in the natural for alcohol to leave our system and sober us up. So, no matter what, we are bound by the effects of what we are intoxicated by.

I've personally experienced a rollercoaster of emotions when I was intoxicated by fear, anger, or hurt. Dwelling on something negative until the emotion hits, only to suffer the consequences of fear and anxiety until the situation passes. Which, in some cases, can be much longer than alcohol. Maybe starting Sunday evening after receiving bad news that causes anxious thinking all week long. Thankfully, with the help of the Holy Spirit, as you will soon see, we can skip the ride of emotion and maintain clarity and wisdom in a situation, even when it is long and painful.

'The natural person does not accept the things of the Spirit of God, for they are folly to him, and he is not able to understand them because they are spiritually discerned. The spiritual person judges all things, but is himself to be judged by no one. "For who has understood the mind of the Lord so as to instruct him?" But we have the mind of Christ.'
1 Corinthians 2:14-16

'The end of all things is at hand; therefore be self-controlled and sober-minded for the sake of your prayers. '
1 Peter 4:7

Our emotions and feelings can get the best of us and leave us as prey for the devil to devour. But if we practice being sober-minded in life, then when the devil comes on the prowl, he won't be able to devour us because we are guarded by a sober mind in Christ, and we remain effective and untouched by pressure. We won't fall into the what-if games, or fears that overwhelm us with constant scenarios of things that may or may not even happen.

Our emotions are so powerful that we can feel as though the thought or scenario has already happened or will happen, and it leaves us emotionally exhausted, confused, lacking clarity or understanding and unaware of the truth in the current situation. We can easily become intoxicated or impaired by circumstances. But the fruit of self-control is where we have a sober mind, and that protects and makes us aware of the devil's prowling. We are not in the off position, comfortable, relaxed or naive to the devil, but we are aware because of the active fruit of self-control working in our life and blessing us and others around us.

Look at what Jesus' brother James says:

'If any of you lacks wisdom, let him ask God, who gives generously to all without reproach, and it will be given him. But let him ask in faith, with no doubting, for the one who doubts is like a wave of the sea that is driven and tossed by the wind. For that person must not

suppose that he will receive anything from the Lord; he is a double-minded man, unstable in all his ways. '
James 1:5-8

Consider what the Scriptures reveal about our emotions; they can limit our thinking, and we can become double-minded and unstable. I have been there before, and it can feel impossible and hopeless. I am thankful God's Word literally has everything we need to overcome difficult situations. Our emotions are not bad; in fact, they are given to us by God, and emotions like love, joy, compassion, sorrow, anger, and grief, to name a few, help us process and enjoy life as well as help us understand and empathize with others. It is important that we do not suppress or ignore our emotions but rather go to God with them to help us walk in self-control and a sober mind. Then we will maintain clarity and understanding not getting trapped by one or more emotions. When we become overwhelmed by negative emotions, our judgment is impaired. Emotions like unrighteous anger, fear, shame, guilt, and uncertainty can debilitate, trigger, or influence our thoughts, feelings, and actions.

Have you ever looked at the ocean to study the waves? Some waves have a steady pattern but still a constant beating, while other waves are all over the place because of a storm that passes through and creates an atmosphere where patterns cannot be predicted; it's just chaos in the sea. Anyone in that storm would be devoured by the waves, tossing you around, beating you without a chance for breath or sight. So much is going on so quickly and unexpectedly that you are drowning, unable to see and literally fighting for your life without knowing how to fight or when to breathe.

You might not be in a literal ocean, but maybe you feel like you are drowning in debt and can't stop the bills from coming. Maybe there is a relational challenge or a betrayal that beats your heart like rough waters. What about a spiritual attack that keeps coming at you with no place for you to find shelter or rest? The storms of life can come unexpectedly, but Jesus always provides a way out. He promises to never leave us or forsake us. He promises that if we keep our eyes on Him instead of the waves, we will walk through the storm and not drown. He calls us to forgive and seek peace in situations where our natural response wants to end things. Jesus is always calling us higher, not alone but in Him.

'So shall they fear the name of the Lord from the west,
And His glory from the rising of the sun;
When the enemy comes in like a flood,
The Spirit of the Lord will lift up a standard against him.'
Isaiah 59:19

The Word says in Isaiah 59 that when the enemy comes in like a flood, the Spirit of the Lord will lift up a standard against the enemy. The standard is the Word, who is Jesus in the flesh. And the Word became flesh and dwelt among us. When we accepted Jesus Christ as Lord and Savior, we were each given a new Spirit in Christ, redeemed and righteous. This new Spirit is how God helps us through the nudging of the Holy Spirit. God is calling us to rise above the storm to His standard and His Word, to a place where we will not be overwhelmed by the storm because we choose not to let our minds or judgment be impaired by the circumstance.

The more I grow in the things of God, the more the Holy Spirit helps me discern situations, and the less I am overcome by the storms of life. Does it mean I am never overcome by a storm? No, but that is the goal. To be so in-tune with the divine nature of God that it becomes mine, and I am not ineffective in my walk on earth, easily being caught up in storms.

This sober mind also helps me guard my witness to others, which is so important and powerful. A place where words don't speak, but our response to a situation does.

'I know how to be brought low, and I know how to abound. In any and every circumstance, I have learned the secret of facing plenty and hunger, abundance and need. I can do all things through Him who strengthens me. '
Philippians 4:12-13

Think about how powerful it would be if you rose above a situation with self-control, a sober mind, and sober judgment. Can you think for a moment what security in your identity looks like? A place where there is freedom from embarrassment, fear, shame, hurt, and not being enough, where you are not feeling anxious talking to someone or sharing your ideas or feelings.

I began asking women in my life serving alongside me and growing in the things of God, what it would look like in their lives to be fully free, lacking nothing, fearing nothing, with the anointing and direction of God clearly going before them... What it would look like to walk out the will of God for their life. Honestly, God wants us to catch a vision for "her" and trust Him to help us walk out that freedom in real time, but it's not without the fruit of self-control. No matter how badly you want change or to rise above, be free, not react, you must cultivate the fruit of self-control. And the good news is you absolutely can, no matter who your parents were, what your past is, or what your natural habit is, God can and will help you if you ask Him to.

Think of how much unity, peace, safety, and forgiveness would be in the Church if we all kept a sober mind. Instead of waiting for an anointed or 'drop the mic' moment in Church or a podcast to stir and convict us, we can begin to pursue a life of spiritual maturity today. That spiritual maturity restores others and is the place where love really does cover a multitude of sins. In Christ, we are able to do all that He asks us, not apart from Him, but because of Him and by the help of the Holy Spirit.

How does this help us with the Local Church? Well, I'm glad you asked. All of our church hurt is people-related, not God-related, even if we or others think it is God related. Unfortunately, someone may have misinformed us or misrepresented God in a situation they lacked understanding or truth in. But the freedom Jesus offers us in the Word is truth and clarity. The Word says the truth will set you free, free from control, feelings, fear, anxiety, and other things that bind us.

The truth Jesus offers us through the Scriptures and His life shows us how to live with a sober mind, full of clarity and understanding, and aware of the enemy's tactics to sow doubt, discord and enmity in the body of Christ. If the enemy can get you to look at people as your real enemy, then he can continue wreaking havoc on your life and limiting the power and strength of The Local Church.

'For by the grace given to me I say to everyone among you not to think of himself more highly than he ought to think, but to think with sober judgment, each according to the measure of faith that God has assigned. '
Romans 12:3

I love this Scripture so much because it's very easy for us to get prideful; in fact, that is the way of the flesh and sin. But the way of the Spirit through sanctification is one of serving others and leading a life of hope. Think of how Jesus washed the feet of Judas, knowing he would betray Him just a few moments later, yet His sober mind allowed for the divine nature to pursue purpose and see the bigger picture, rather than being hurt and limited by the betrayal.

Where would we all be if Jesus would have reacted to Judas and stopped being obedient to the Father because someone betrayed Him and He allowed it to stop Him? I'm so thankful He did not. Who is on the other side of your obedience to the Father? My sweet friend, do not let anyone get in the way with their hurtful actions and stop you. Others are counting on your faithfulness to God!

Like we saw earlier, the opposite of sober is intoxication, and if we are not sober in mind or judgment, then our mind and judgment will be impaired by what intoxicates them. Anger, fear, comparison, anxiety, hate, you name it. We don't want to let any of those things impair our minds and judgment. The word "impair" means to weaken or damage. Think back to 1 Peter 5:8, the devil, our real enemy, is on the prowl for weakened or damaged prey. In nature, when an animal is weakened or has damaged a part of its body, it's just a matter of time before a predator comes to devour it.

Let's guard our hearts and minds and not be quick to take offense, but rather quick to forgive and seek peace with others.

"If possible, so far as it depends on you, live peaceably with all. Beloved, never avenge yourselves, but leave it to the wrath of God, for it is written, "Vengeance is mine, I will repay, says the Lord." To the contrary, "if your enemy is hungry, feed him; if he is thirsty, give him something to drink; for by so doing you will heap burning coals on his head." Do not be overcome by evil, but overcome evil with good.'
Romans 12:18-21

Like you, I can think of many times when I was hurt or offended. Many times, where they were wrong and I was right. But because they were wrong, my flesh convinced me that I had the right to end the relationship, judge them, dishonor them, or even not be obedient to God. I couldn't do it anymore because it wasn't fair, or they would never receive from me, or they might not change... sound familiar? Well, just because we feel we have the right to stop or dismiss them does not mean we should act on it. Quite the opposite, let's lavish others with forgiveness and seek peace because we cultivated self-control. Let's love one another with the same love lavished over us and stir one another on to good works.

Let's be as wise as the enemy but as gentle as a dove. Let's protect the Church not with hurt that impairs our judgment but with love and peace that guards our heart, mind, and soul.

TIME TO REFLECT AND REJECT

Can you think of a time when a sober mind would have saved you from the emotional exhaustion of being impaired by what was happening?

_____

_____

_____

_____

_____

_____

Have you experienced a moment when your witness in a situation blessed others more than your words?

_____

_____

_____

_____

_____

_____

Do you see the enemy as your real enemy instead of God's precious people? How can you now position yourself in a posture of wisdom and clarity by not succumbing to the ways of the flesh?

_____

_____

_____

_____

_____

_____

When someone says or does something hurtful, how do you respond? Do you respond in honor and in peace, or are you quick to react, casting judgment and exposing their sin, or justifying yourself because you were offended or hurt?

_____

_____

_____

_____

_____

_____

What would it look like to catch a vision of "her"? To be fully free, lacking nothing, fearing nothing, with the anointing and direction of God clearly going before you? What could it look like to walk out the will of God for your life?

_____
_____
_____
_____
_____
_____

Now that you've learned the divine benefits of a sober mind and self-control, how can you use these gifts to protect the unity and camaraderie of your local Church?

_____
_____
_____
_____
_____
_____

Ask God to help you guard your emotions and keep them in check with a sober mind and sober judgment. Ask God to help you rise above the flesh in moments that call for spiritual wisdom to protect His Church, keeping a safe and authentic place of faith, hope, and love.

A Prayer For You

Heavenly Father, I thank you for this beloved woman reading this bible study. I thank you for helping her grow in the fruit of the Spirit, so that self-control is plentiful in her life. I speak truth over her in the name of Jesus, and that you, Lord, would help her resist the lies of the enemy as well as the lies of her flesh. Lord, reveal what only the Holy Spirit can and help her recognize the power and strength she has in Christ. Heal her and give her the lens of grace to see others the way you see them, as well as the spiritual discernment to recognize the spiritual war at hand. In Jesus' name.

YOU BELONG
WEEK 3

YOU BELONG
Week 3

You belong in the house of God, not alone.
A call to wake up in love!

The Great Commission

'And Jesus came and said to them, "All authority in heaven and on earth has been given to me. Go therefore and make disciples of all nations, baptizing them in the name of the Father and of the Son and of the Holy Spirit, teaching them to observe all that I have commanded you. And behold, I am with you always, to the end of the age."'
Matthew 28:18-20

Jesus is coming back, the only thing is we don't know exactly when. But we do know we will see signs leading up to His coming. Some have already begun as the day draws near, and the Bible says the earth will groan with natural disasters, war, and moral decline, among other things. I don't share this to scare you; I share this to stir you into action. The local church is the hope of the world. Believers boldly proclaiming the Good News of Jesus Christ, not just through word but by love and action.

The truth is, there are many people in the world who still do not know the saving knowledge of Jesus Christ, and some of them are closer than you think. Oftentimes, our minds go to remote places or underdeveloped nations, but right here in America, more and more people do not know anything about God or even who Jesus Christ is. Let that sink in for a moment.

If we don't place a high value on the body of Christ— the Local Church— we will limit our reach as believers together. The enemy and our flesh cause us to focus on ourselves, hurt, or the hypocrisy of others, which over time limits who we are uniquely created to be. This causes us to withdraw from the body entirely or to church hop, never being fully planted and never experiencing what it is to flourish in the local body. More on that later...

This stirring I am challenging you with is to wake up to the reality of the spiritual warfare against believers effectively accomplishing the Great Commission. This warfare begins in a place we cannot see with the natural eye and manifests in the natural through the flesh. For us to effectively accomplish the Great Commission that Jesus left us with, we have to wake up from the slumber of society, offence, hurry and selfishness. We cannot stay bound to these things if we want to do His will effectively.

So many things get us distracted or offended, even a life of ease will distract you leaving you unaware of the spiritual battle at hand. We've looked at grace and a sober mind, things we cultivate in the washing of the Word and proximity to Jesus. Now we will take a look at love in action. Waking up with awareness to be available, notice, pause, practice and pray in the power we have received from God through Jesus by the help of the Holy Spirit in you.

You don't need to be a pastor or elder to have significant influence or to have this power, it is already available for you to walk in. Our flesh tries to tell us that because we are not seen on a platform or we don't speak or sing well, God can't really use us in the scheme of things, and our gift is not that important in the church. But what a horrible lie that is from the pit of hell, meant to immediately devalue and dim you in the body of Christ.

As we will see in a moment, faithfulness in love to anything we do for God will not be in vain. But anything we do for God and the church, no matter how wonderful and impactful it looks or could be, if it is not in love, it is pointless and just loud obnoxious noise. You my dear friend as a believer and daughter of the Most High are of great value in the Body of Christ and before you can even do anything for the Kingdom you are God's beloved child in whom He is well pleased. Not because of what you can do but because of what Jesus Christ already did for you to put you in perfect standing with God the Father. You belong in His Church, you have a powerful part to play in the body of Christ whether it is seen or unseen, glamorous or quiet. God sees your faithfulness, and He is the true rewarder, not man.

Our flesh, the culture and influence of a fallen world, and our real enemy, the devil, are counting on us being proud, lacking identity, taking offense, being judgmental, not forgiving, throwing stones, isolating, and more. But when we were saved, we weren't given the Spirit of the world; we were given the Spirit of the living God. We are new creations in Christ Jesus; the old has passed away, and God has made all things new in you. That is the truth, and every day we need to walk in that new creation and allow the beautiful and powerful work of sanctification to take place in our lives through the washing of the Word and proximity to the Father.

We need to wake up from the slumber of our pain or fears and cast them to the Lord, for He cares for us. Do you hear me, sweet friend, wake up from the heaviness of whatever burdens or stops you and cast the care to your Lord and Savior. You belong in the church, not because you are perfect, but because you've been redeemed by perfect love, restored and filled with purpose. It's that grace again: unearned, unmerited and God wants to unveil His good plan to you and for you as you walk out the great commission in your life.

Who the Son sets free is free indeed. The Body of Christ is precious and powerful. A place of healing and freedom. A place where you grow in the image of Christ with other believers, and together you are stirring each other on to good works and caring for each other's needs. A place of support and not judgment. A place of accountability and championing. Together we are fulfilling the body of Christ, some a finger, some a heart, some feet and ribs, and others the veins that carry blood. We each play a vital part in the body of Christ, and for the body to function effectively, it must not diminish or devalue any of its members nor lack love.

This passage here in Romans helps us look at the gifts with a broader and more impactful perspective. Not putting a title on something or someone but valuing each gift and prompting action.

'For as in one body we have many members, and the members do not all have the same function, so we, though many, are one body in Christ, and individually members one of another. Having gifts that differ according to the grace given to us, let us use them: if prophecy, in proportion to our faith; if service, in our serving; the one who teaches, in his teaching; the one who exhorts, in his exhortation; the one who contributes, in generosity; the one who leads, with zeal; the one who does acts of mercy, with cheerfulness. Let love be genuine. Abhor what is evil; hold fast to what is good. Love one another with brotherly affection. Outdo one another in showing honor. '
Romans 12:4-10

Wow, right! No part is diminished or devalued in this beautiful reminder that if you have a gift (not a title), then you should operate in it fully, confidently and without comparison. If you have a gift of mercy, but you keep comparing your gift to someone who has a leadership gifting, then you won't be able to confidently and fully operate in the mercy with cheerfulness. Don't let the enemy devalue you when you get saved, and don't let comparison rob you of living in purpose, fully content and valued.

'Now you are the body of Christ and individually members of it. And God has appointed in the church first apostles, second prophets, third teachers, then miracles, then gifts of healing, helping, administrating, and various kinds of tongues. Are all apostles? Are all prophets? Are all teachers? Do all work miracles? Do all possess gifts of healing? Do all speak with tongues? Do all interpret? But earnestly desire the higher gifts. And I will show you a still more excellent way.'   1 Corinthians 12:27-31

What is this more excellent way? You will soon see in 1 Corinthians 13, and I pray that as you read through this incredible inspired Word of God, understanding will begin to illuminate in your spirit, and you will walk out all that you do, not in vain, but in complete purpose and fully effective!

I want to preface this, too: Chapter 13 is a portion of a larger letter written to a church addressing issues such as conflict, pride, sexual immorality, and lawsuits against other believers (and if you've ever seen a lawsuit usually greed or betrayal is involved)— and a few other things. Paul is also writing this hungry, thirsty, poorly dressed, and homeless, yet the Spirit of God at work in his life is producing fruit that will not perish, and as we read this passage, we get to eat this fruit together and let it nourish our spirits and stir us towards good works. Let's begin.

'If I speak in the tongues of men and of angels, but have not love, I am a noisy gong or a clanging cymbal. And if I have prophetic powers, and understand all mysteries and all knowledge, and if I have all faith, so as to remove mountains, but have not love, I am nothing. If I give away all I have, and if I deliver up my body to be burned, but have not love, I gain nothing. Love is patient and kind; love does not envy or boast; it is not arrogant or rude. It does not insist on its own way; it is not irritable or resentful; it does not rejoice at wrongdoing, but rejoices with the truth. Love bears all things, believes all things, hopes all things, endures all things. Love never ends. As for prophecies, they will pass away; as for tongues, they will cease; as for knowledge, it will pass away. For we know in part and we prophesy in part, but when the perfect comes, the partial will pass away. When I was a child, I spoke like a child, I thought like a child, I reasoned like a child. When I became a man, I gave up childish ways. For now we see in a mirror

dimly, but then face to face. Now I know in part; then I shall know fully, even as I have been fully known. So now faith, hope, and love abide, these three; but the greatest of these is love.'
1 Corinthians 13:1-13

We need to wake up from the deception of our flesh, puffing us up, clinging to offense, resisting the body of Christ, and leaving us dead and disconnected from each other. We are the body of Christ together, not alone.

"They overcame by the blood of the lamb and the word of their testimony. Revelation 12:11

Together we are fellow citizens with the saints, and members of God's house. Ephesians 2:19

'Where two or more are gathered there, He is in the midst of them". Matthew 18:20

Prayer of agreement where two or more people link their faith according to God's will. Matthew 18:19

Do you see this? You belong. Let me say it again, you belong in the house of God, in the body of Christ. Together we fulfill the Great Commission, together we reach our communities and affect generational change through the ways of God. The Lord is at work in the plural of peoples: they, their, fellow, them, agree....

Commit to waking up with me to the truth and not being deceived by the flesh. You belong in the effective reach of the local church, and together we are better.

You can do all things through Christ who strengthens you. You can forgive, you can restore, you can release, you can humble yourself, you can be obedient to God and walk out your calling faithfully in Christ. Not in yourself but in Christ, and as you do this, your influence will grow bright, you will shine bright in the darkness, drawing the lost and pointing them to Christ. And the best part is Jesus' promise to you, that He will be with you to the end of the age.

"The harvest is full, but the laborers are few. Pray to the Lord of the harvest to send laborers."

My dear friend, you are on the other side of my prayer. I pray that at the end of this, you run into the fields with purpose in love and help restore the harvest to the Father. You are a Local Church Girl, and God is filling you with fresh wind. Step out in faith and trust His process, trust His plan fully. His plans are higher and are only limited by our hesitation or fear of trusting Him. He is good, there is no evil in Him.

TIME TO REFLECT AND REJECT

Have you ever felt like you weren't that important in the body of Christ and why?

_____

_____

_____

_____

_____

_____

Have you allowed comparison to steal your obedience and value?

_____

_____

_____

_____

_____

_____

Like Paul writes in 1 Corinthians 13 giving us insight and greater detail to our effectiveness as believers, do you need to adjust how you have operated in the past without love? Have you been loud like a "noisy gong" ineffective in your speech, calling and character? Ask God to help you so that Love leads everything you do, say and think.

_____

_____

_____

_____

_____

_____

Did you make a commitment to wake up and see the truth?

_____

_____

_____

_____

_____

_____

What did the Spirit reveal to you?

_____

_____

_____

_____

_____

Do you have some burdens, hurt, or fear you need to give to the Lord? Ask Him to show you how much He cares for you, and that you can give these things to Him knowing He will help you.

_____

_____

_____

_____

_____

_____

PEOPLE PLEASING OR PLEASING GOD

WEEK 4

PEOPLE PLEASEING OR PLEASEING GOD
Week 4

Codependency in the church.
If we are trying to please man, we are not servants of Christ but servants to our flesh.

Codependency in the church may not look like how we normally understand it. The definition of codependency is an unhealthy emotional attachment to someone rooted in low self-esteem and a strong desire for approval, sometimes by controlling or manipulative people or those who enable behavior, usually without realizing it. Looking at this in definition form, it is wrong, and some of us would even say we don't struggle with that. But what if I challenged you to take a deeper look?

I had to take a deeper look and step back from my own life to see how I had, in fact, had a few codependent relationships in the church. It wasn't easy for me to see right off the bat; I'm in my thirties, and I've just noticed this. I was one of those people who said "No, I don't deal with that". But I want to share this part of my life with you to help you recognize it and either prevent it from happening or stop it if it is actively happening. Codependency on anyone, even amazing leaders, is still wrong because none of us are perfect, completely available, and worthy to be dependent on.

Only Jesus is, and we want to help others, especially with wounds or traumas, turn to Jesus for all they need, to be completely dependent on Him. He is worthy and able to save, heal, and restore.

As I mentioned earlier, I was saved at fourteen and quickly got planted in my local church, the same church where I later became a pastor. The problem is, I was deeply wounded and going through a difficult season in my life. My parents, though they loved me, were both consumed with success and struggling with their marriage. My father replicated an unhealthy familial culture, and my mom, though she was sweet and happy, was unable to confront my father's behavior and didn't know how to comfort us. I ended up trying to earn my dad's love and value, which led me to a life of earning and proving; some would call perfectionism.

When I started serving at the church, I clung to my now mother-in-love, who was my senior pastor, and over time, I unknowingly became dependent on her opinion and approval, almost as if she were giving me permission to be the real me. She was kind, wise, and caring, and it seemed like there was always time for me when I needed it. I'm sure clinging to her had a lot to do with Chris, my now husband, lol.

This unhealthy attachment happened again after many years of rotating friends who used, betrayed, judged, labeled, and gossiped about me. I didn't know how to discern real godly friends because I was so desperate to be wanted. Look at this oxymoron— I met my best friend, Rae, and we hit it off amazingly until she called to tell me how much she liked me and thought we could be best friends. I froze on the phone and said Yeah, of course, but I never called her back for at least a year. For me, it was too much pressure to live up to something so good, and I thought I couldn't have what she said we had. Thankfully, she was busy and about to get married, so I quietly hung out around her while I kept the other friends in my life who were familiar but not God's best for me.

Time went on, and our closeness grew until one day we were best friends for real. I don't remember when it quite happened, but I'm thankful it did.

As I grew in leadership, my insecurities and lack of identity became more apparent, though I was blind to it. Plus, the unresolved and added hurt from more people compounded by my inability to stop the cycle or even notice it, only made things worse. Even though I was saved, I had no idea how to use what God had given me to live free and full of identity. I needed deep heart work.

I started not trusting anyone but Rae. She was the one who saw most of the betrayal and walked with me through it. So naturally, I began to cling to her familiarity, safety, and aid instead of going to God for safety and aid. The familiarity I clung to was a form of safety I thought I had in those friends who weren't God's best for me, but also in one of my older friendships from middle school. She was strong, caring, and seemed unafraid of anyone or anything. I would call her when my dad overreacted, and she would comfort me and had a righteous anger that made me feel safe, seen, and understood. We ended up drifting apart the older we got, and then I had no one in my corner anymore.

When Rae and I became close friends, I found the same kind of strong, caring, and righteous anger in her. She was loyal, faithful, and a gift from God to me. Something about Rae was different than the others, but my past experience told me I could not have it. I began seeing a pattern in the kinds of women I was drawn to. Though they had some good qualities, there were red flags in them that I minimized because my wounds were familiar to them.

I've learned through this refining in my life that God wants to be the first and last person I run to for safety, healing, and identity, that He already sees me, and that I am fully known in Him. Refinement is sometimes looked at with a fearful perspective. The idea of being put in the fire to draw out the impurities scares many of us, so we avoid this refinement for years, not knowing it is actually intended for our healing, strengthening, and to discover our true identity, the one that the Master sees and intends for us.

When we allow the Lord to refine us like silver in the flame, He carefully watches over us not to burn, as the impurities rise to the surface where He is then able to remove them from our lives like they never existed before.

Can you imagine having a wound, trauma, false belief, or manipulation of the truth removed and healed from you like it never happened? Maybe you were in an abusive relationship or abandoned. Perhaps you were criticized often, or neglected, and forced to care for yourself at a young age. Many painful things can trap us in unhealthy patterns of self-protection. Again, I want to remind you to trust God with your wounds; with Him, you can safely find freedom and restoration. Little by little, we begin to bear His image each time He takes us out of the flame. The only way to know when silver is completely pure is when the refiner can see His image clearly reflected.

God has a righteous anger to protect and save, and it's only limited by our thinking but expanded in His power and faithfulness when we trust Him fully. Abuse and manipulation in children are difficult places to mend, but I can tell you firsthand that God has restored my foundation through His loving and faithful process. Going to a friend rather than God is a cycle that may help for a season but may not guarantee the freedom you so desperately need. The Lord is the most skillful and perfect refiner in all of creation. He knit you once before; He is faithful to mend your life and see you through. Nothing is too hard for Him.

Thank God both my mother-in-love and bestie were not manipulative. I know God used them to help me heal, but again, some of the help I needed was something only God could do within me. I needed my heavenly Father to refine me by rebuilding a foundation laid with impurities and hollow space. It took careful excavation and trusting His process, not mine.

Let's take a look at crutches; they aid your mobility after injury for a short season so that we can regain full mobility. However, if we no longer need them and do not transition away from them at the proper time, they will become a hindrance to the user. Your body can atrophy, losing muscle mass, strength, and endurance. This weakening unnecessarily burdens other areas, developing bruising or new sores unrelated to the original injury. Instead of a temporary aid as they were designed, they become a necessity because we cannot function without their help. Our ability to use that wounded limb as it was originally designed is now lost, and we become comfortable with the limitation or fear. Our confidence can only be fully affirmed in who we are in Christ, and lingering in fear or pain will only put limitations on us. The mighty Word of God says that perfect love casts out fear. (1 John 4:18)

I want to be clear, people can absolutely help us heal and affirm our identity, actions, fruit, and the path we are taking, but some of the more sensitive or hidden wounds in our life can only be restored by our heavenly Father through Jesus and the help of the Holy Spirit. I did atrophy in who I was after all the hurt, I lost mass, strength and endurance, I even developed other wounds unrelated to the original injury. Thankfully, when I needed it most, God created space for me to lean into His counsel and find healing. This did not happen overnight, but it was years of unpacking pain with Him and a wonderful Christian counselor God placed in my life. God saw the cycle I was trapped in and offered a way out. I'm so glad I took it and was completely covered in God's grace to begin truly healing in Him.

Coping skills are another form of temporary help in managing stressful situations or uncomfortable emotions, such as anxiety or frustration. However, they do expire over time, as they too are meant to be brief. Something that was once helpful and intended to be temporary until change comes can become useless as help or unhealthy. There are some coping skills like exercise, warm baths, picking up a fun hobby, or reading that are positive and helpful, but if the change does not come, hopelessness can start to fill our hearts, leading to weariness. Have you ever found yourself in a repeating cycle where change does not come? It can definitely leave you weary and lacking the ability to hope.

There are also negative coping skills like overeating, sleeping too much, venting, avoiding, retail therapy, or drug and alcohol abuse that are harmful and blind us to or suppress the root issue. We aren't meant to be stuck in anxiety or frustration, minimizing or masking them. We need healing and help to make changes. God knows just how to help. He is the perfect Father, with no hidden agenda or manipulation, only good and faithful to see us through. His ways lead to a good and secure life. Everything Jesus endured on the cross was for our peace, and by His wounds we are healed (Isaiah 53:5). Not just physically, but emotionally as well. Right here, right now, wherever you are, you can pause and ask God to help you begin healing in areas you may have been blind to for years.

Deep Breath

'"Blessed is the man who trusts in the Lord, whose trust is the Lord. '
Jeremiah 17:7

'for the Lord will be your confidence and will keep your foot from being caught. '
Proverbs 3:26

' Trust in the Lord, and do good; dwell in the land and befriend faithfulness. Delight yourself in the Lord, and he will give you the

desires of your heart. Commit your way to the Lord; trust in him, and he will act. He will bring forth your righteousness as the light, and your justice as the noonday. Be still before the Lord and wait patiently for him; fret not yourself over the one who prospers in his way, over the man who carries out evil devices! '
Psalm 37:3-7

Have you ever studied the story of King Saul, Israel's first-ever king? In Saul's journey, we see someone who has all the outward signs of a great leader: young, handsome, wealthy, coming from a good family, including the psychology of height, (LOL I can relate, I'm 6'1).

The Bible recounts him being taller than all the people from his shoulders up. He was even given a new heart by God (1 Samuel 10:9), yet he never learned how to rely on God for confidence and his self-esteem, even after the Spirit of the Lord rushed upon him and he prophesied. Instead, he relied on who he was instead of cultivating who God was anointing him to be. This left him overwhelmed by what was being entrusted to him, and he ended up hiding in the baggage during his own coronation.

As you study the story of King Saul, you see that soon enough, he makes a big mistake, and instead of waiting on the Lord and honoring the position of the prophet Samuel, he stepped out in disobedience because of fear. A fear that God gave him every opportunity to be free from. In turn, we read this line **"I feared the people and obeyed their voice."** (1 Samuel 15:24). What is sad is that the prophet Samuel instructed King Saul before his big mistake saying **"Only fear the Lord and serve Him faithfully with all your heart"** (1 Samuel 12:24). This is a form of codependency to the people at large. People pleasing because of a lack of identity and the deception of popularity rather than pleasing God. King Saul was ultimately unable to make the people wait because of the pressure he felt from them, and he was fearful of their rejection and their opinion of him.

Saul grew up learning to rely on his outward qualities. These were the things he put his hope in, and unfortunately, when he received more wealth, a bigger name, and the whole kingdom, it crippled him rather than blessing him and the people he was called to lead (not take orders from). When we serve God above others, we naturally serve people for their best interest in God's will, but when we serve people above God, we actually reject God —even if our intentions are good. Our will, will never be as good as God's will. Don't let your intentions limit God's goodness even if you don't see the big picture. If we are not careful, we will teach our kids to value the appearance of success, which fades away, chasing it rather than valuing God's instruction to true success. Learning to wait on the Lord is a powerful fruit of the spirit. Many times, delay is spiritual warfare, and the only way to recognize it is to be developed spiritually.

The anointing of "king" was then taken from Saul and given to a lowly, meek shepherd boy who had none of the external lures of success. Even his standing in his own home was overlooked when the prophet Samuel was looking for a new king to anoint among his brothers, all of whom were called by his father except for David. Yet there was something very special about David that God could use radically; it was his confidence and faith in God, not himself or his family. Did you catch that? David was called by his God, not his earthly father. If we are not careful, we will allow people to call us and approve us rather than God, who has already done both. As you read the incredible story of David, you begin to see the hidden character that God was able to use. Someone who was already faithful to God and never needed a new heart. His heart had already been cultivated through his life, drawing close to God. David didn't need his family's approval to be obedient to the God who called and anointed him nor their affirmation, though it happened right in front of their eyes. No, as we now know, David was known as a man after God's own heart, not people and not himself.

We are more like King Saul than we want to admit, but we have a choice to make. Will we surrender to God or man? David was hurt by his own family, and yet God restored and refreshed his spirit because he took refuge in God and not in others or himself.

I wonder how you relate? How can you begin to run to your Heavenly Father before you run to others, even if they are safe? How can you practice the things David did that made him dependent on God? Things that made him a man who did not need a new heart because his heart was already set on the things of God.

As a young shepherd boy, David regularly sought the Lord in prayer and worship and was a faithful servant in the field, tending to his father's sheep. He even looked at God as his own shepherd in Psalm 23 and said things like **"I shall not want"** and **"He leads me in paths of righteousness for His name's sake."** These are the kinds of things he said and meditated on before he was crowned King. He was not proud but humble, and God sought him out for kingship, not the other way around. Later in the Psalms, we see David cry out to God for help and protection as his enemy, King Saul, hunted him down. David shows that he is honorable even in hidden places. There was a moment in a cave when he could have ended King Saul's life and finally become king. But we see David honor God's office of authority rather than his own honor and was unwilling to sin against God to attain what God had anointed him for.

Prayer, worship, humility, and honor may not seem like the kind of leadership qualities you need to rule a nation, but to the Lord, they are what He loves to use. God resists the proud and draws near to the humble. It's worth noting that David knew God as his Lord, and now, because of Jesus, we are sons and daughters of God and can approach Him as our Heavenly Father. We may not be called by our earthly parents or the people we think we should be noticed by, but we are called by our heavenly Father through Christ.

We've looked at codependency for a reason in this chapter —it is deep heart work, and it is a revealer. Who you are dependent on reveals who you are faithfully committed to. We will let others down, and others will let us down. We will sin and miss the mark, and others will too. Our dependency needs to be on God. It's not a matter of if we will get hurt; it's a matter of when, and when we get hurt, who we cling to will decide if we stay faithfully planted in the house of God or not.

I know this can be heavy, especially if you have been hurt and have left the local body. There may be other reasons why you left that are unrelated to codependency. Don't miss this part. We become more and more dependent on God through sanctification. We don't want to allow a lack of identity or value to hurt or confuse us, hindering our growth and calling. I was hindered by low self-esteem, lack of identity, and kept my fears hidden from others, thinking I was protected, even though everything I did had traces of pain. However, the real trap was that I wasn't walking in the freedom Jesus had already paid for me, something I did not need to earn and was already valued enough for Him to embrace the cross for. Instead, I was stuck and crippled by the fears until I had to make a choice. Am I obedient to fear, people, or God?

This question helped me surrender fully to God and trust Him as He was asking me to step out in faith. One day, I was painting my toenails and complaining to my Husband and God, trying to justify why I couldn't be fully obedient, when all of a sudden, the name of my nail polish gripped me, **"Enuf is Enuf"**. At that moment, the Holy Spirit arrested my heart and said, **"Are you going to be obedient to God or your feelings? You can forgive that person, and you can be obedient and step out in all that I've asked you."**

I can't tell you how many times in the past I wanted to stop going to church because I was hurt or fearful of others. I even thought, "Oh, I'll just go somewhere else and not be hurt," or I'll leave very kindly so that it does not hurt the church, and I can be okay". But those were not godly solutions to the real issues. Even if we leave but don't address the pain or our lack of identity, we are doomed to repeat the cycle. God has given us every tool to heal, forgive, and restore our identity, helping us stay rooted and flourish together in His body. Looking back at the early church in Acts, we see the beauty of the "great grace" that was upon all the people who had all things in common because of their complete surrender to God's ways and love for one another. I want to challenge you to check your heart. Where do others have a hold on your faithfulness to God?

We can all buy into the lie that we don't "need" the church, that we are good people, justifying things we do to stay close to God, or help people we are comfortable with helping. But again, we do need the church, and the world needs the church. Not an earthly church, but a heavenly one that God is using to make His kingdom known on earth as it is in heaven. We were made for community, not isolation. God Himself commands a blessing on unity, and by this unity, the love that we have for one another, others will be added to the church, not because of hype but because of the testimony of Jesus Christ's work in our lives. Our youth Pastor says this often, "like a moth to a flame."

The Apostle Paul is a wonderful example of being a servant or slave to Christ and not fear, hurt, others, selfishness, self-preservation, or even his past. And if you know anything about Paul's history before Christ transformed him, you would see why it could be easy to let his past limit him, but it didn't because Paul refused to identify or boast about who he was. He only boasted in what God was doing in him. Our flesh tries to do a few things to us even though we are in Christ. It tries to diminish us because of our fears and insecurity, our past, and even people's value or opinion of us. It also tries to puff us up, so we think we are highly important and have a self-righteous approach towards others rather than a heart of servitude, grace, and hope.

Let's ask the Lord to search our hearts, not for punishment but for healing and strengthening. Partial obedience is not true obedience. Let's teach others to run to God first while we support and cheer them on. Let's become faithful like David and Paul, who knew who they were and needed no man to approve them. Remember, we are called and anointed by God, not people. This guards our identity when shame, people's opinions, or persecution arise, and what happens is that we remain faithful even when others are not.

TIME TO REFLECT AND REJECT

Where are you seeking affirmation and approval from? Is it someone or even a title or gift you operate in?

_____

_____

_____

_____

_____

_____

Have you ever had an experience like King Saul, where you made a decision based on pressure from others rather than trusting and waiting on the Lord?

_____

_____

_____

_____

_____

_____

Where do others have a hold on your faithfulness or obedience to God?

_____

_____

_____

_____

_____

_____

Have you misunderstood the role of the church in believers' lives and the world?

_____

_____

_____

_____

_____

_____

Have you allowed others to ease your wounds rather than going to God first?

_____

_____

_____

_____

_____

_____

How can you begin to allow God to heal you and reveal to you your true identity in him?

_____

_____

_____

_____

_____

_____

COMPETITION OR CLOSNESS
WEEK 5

COMPETITION OR CLOSENESS
Week 5

I'm not here for competition; I'm here for closeness.

The flesh places value on the gift or talent. Love places value on people.

Have you ever felt like others didn't like you or labeled you without taking the time to get to know you? Ever felt unnoticed or as though you were an inconvenience, overshadowed or diminished, reaching for connection and instead rejected? Most of us have experienced some part of this, and these moments can deeply wound us, tear at our sense of identity, and make us feel as though we don't belong, creating questions and doubt about ourselves and how others could perceive us. Maybe we have a strong personality and are a little raw, maybe we are shy, and it's incredibly hard for us to reach out for community. Perhaps we've been wounded, and we can't step out because we are crippled by fear. I want to encourage and love on you for a moment and remind you whose you are.

You, my dear friend, are a child of the Most High King. The Word says He knew you before He knit you in your mother's womb. He calls you beloved and has uniquely formed your body, mind, and soul. You are of great value, and there is a wonderful journey ahead of you to fulfill all that God has for you, including your healing and freedom. You are fully known.

It is not an accident that you picked up this study. It is on purpose to remind you whose you are and to restore and rebuild your identity, not in yourself, but in the Lord, giving you purpose in His Body, the local church. Those who trust in the Lord will not be put to shame. God has given us a Helper who we've talked about throughout the past weeks. That helper is the Holy Spirit, and dear friend, it is the love of God that draws you to repentance and transformation in Christ. So, if you have ever experienced any of the above, Jesus came to set you on a path that would lead to your full freedom as well as others'. This book is not only for you but for the many lives you will influence. I believe with all my heart that those who are found find others, and this brings freedom for generations to come.

I'm not here for competition; I'm here for closeness. This is something I found myself saying. Social media and our high-speed culture have deceived us into self-promotion, not necessarily at the expense of others, but at the expense of ourselves. Feeling the need to do more, be more, and have more. This culture is robbing and trapping us. We become unavailable in this toxic atmosphere, bound by its rules and values rather than God's. So, how do we slow down and resist the tone that has been set, something we may even have been deeply connected to? Honestly, it's through the body of Christ. I love how Paul describes it in Ephesians 4:1-16

'I therefore, a prisoner for the Lord, urge you to walk in a manner worthy of the calling to which you have been called, with all humility and gentleness, with patience, **bearing with one another in love, eager to maintain the unity of the Spirit in the bond of peace.** There is one body and one Spirit—just as you were called to the one hope that belongs to your call— one Lord, one faith, one baptism, one God and Father of all, who is over all and through all and in all. But grace was given to each one of us according to the measure of Christ's gift. Therefore it says, "When he ascended on high he led a host of captives, and he gave gifts to men." (In saying, "He ascended," what does it mean but that he had also descended into the lower regions, the earth? He who descended is the one who also ascended far above all the heavens, that he might fill all things.) And he gave the apostles, the prophets, the evangelists, the shepherds and teachers, **to equip the saints for the work of ministry, for building up the body of Christ,** until we all attain to the unity of the faith and of the knowledge of the Son of God, to mature manhood, to the measure of the stature of the fullness of Christ, so that we may no longer be children, tossed to and fro by the waves and carried about by every wind of doctrine, by human cunning, by craftiness in deceitful schemes. **Rather, speaking the truth in love, we are to grow up in every way into him who is the head, into Christ,**

from whom the whole body, joined and held together by every joint with which it is equipped, when each part is working properly, makes the body grow so that it builds itself up in love. '

This passage of Scripture is packed full of purpose and clarity for individuals and the body of Christ as a whole. Many things we have already touched on are coming together in unity. God uses the church, "the body of Christ," to equip believers for the work of the gospel and for building up the body of Christ. All the gifts and talents God gives us are not for our own glory but for His, through His church, through His Son. We have nothing God hasn't given us. Look at how the tree bears fruit in season. Not for itself but for those who gather to receive fruit from it, close in proximity. Fruit that refreshes, nourishes, and sustains life.

My sweet friend, we are gatherers, and as you read, Christ joins us in love, gathering us to form the whole body with Him, no part overlooked, diminished or labeled, not manipulated or overvalued. Christ is the head of the church, bringing us together, each part working properly. Our flesh and the world place value on the wrong things, diminishing or distorting God's design and intent. But today, right here, right now, I believe He is restoring value and revealing truth to you about His precious church.

Look at how a hair clip gathers hair to create a look with intention and purpose. Similarly, we, as Local Church Girls, gather women together with intention and a heavenly purpose. Intentionally not to miss a woman, to remind her she is seen, found, called, and beloved, full of value and with purpose for her soul to be saved and her family reached. For her life to be unbound, for her stirring, and to cheer her on in the things of God. But we are unable to gather souls when we are carrying the pain, fear, and rejection we've gathered over the years. Today is a new day, with new mercies and grace to help you release the unnecessary weight of things that weigh us down and keep us from being fully effective in Christ.

Let me remind you of the true race we run. It is a spiritual race with the prize of the upward call in Christ, and our flesh cannot run in the same direction the Lord calls and leads us. The flesh can only distract us, limiting our focus and purpose in Christ. To take our eyes off the big picture of redemption and focus on frustrations, offenses and annoyances. These burdens and distractions gathered in our hearts, minds, and souls limit our momentum and effectiveness. The goal of this race is not to be the first amongst each other for boasting, but to press into our individual charge from God with full momentum in faithfulness to God, not our flesh or those who surround us. This race we run has an imperishable prize and genuine joy at the end.

When we release all the things that limit us to the Lord, we release unnecessary weight that only causes weariness. Not only that but look at how social media and the high pace of the world cause us to naturally look at others to compare ourselves and slow us down. Distracting us with what looks like success, to do more, be more, and have more. And if we take the bait of comparison, we begin trying to produce that success in our own life, but most of the time without the grace or anointing to see it through.

Runners cannot focus on other runners while running effectively. No, a good runner is wholly focused on their race; even the slightest wondering if someone is coming to pass them will hinder their present ability. Let us learn to celebrate and not be distracted by each other. We each have a race, and we need to train and prepare according to our needs in Christ, not others' needs. Spending time with the Lord will help you recognize your specific needs as well as your strengths.

There is one more thing we need to address this week, and it is the eagerness to maintain unity. How do we do that with deep wounds and trust issues? How do we open our hearts again when others have not been kind and thoughtful of us? When we've been diminished, manipulated, labeled, or even given up on? When pride leads, and there is an atmosphere of comparison and competition rather than celebration and great joy when others succeed?

Eagerness is a longing, yearning, or wanting something very much; it sounds hopeful, right? Actually, it is, and in Christ through His grace, we can be hopeful. Not because of wishful thinking or living blindly believing the best, on the contrary, we have the power of God at work in our lives and at the tip of our tongue. Instead of giving up or saying things like "this is hopeless" or "they will never change". We can do things like these below to help us pursue peace and unity by the way we pray, speak, and act before others or behind closed doors.

We can intercede through fervent prayer with the help of the Holy Spirit to pray for victory and help in the situation.

We can thank God for peace and unity in our churches and shut down discord and the work of the enemy, but we have to do it. We can't just wish for it to happen or hope it changes on its own. We literally have the power as believers to speak Jesus over the situation and see hearts changed and eyes opened. In this, we are eagerly pursuing and maintaining unity.

Another way is through our actions. It's time to make the first move. Many of us are waiting for others to come to us and say sorry or for closure to happen before we open up or step out in obedience. "Enuf is Enuf", you can do this in Christ. You can be the first to do what is right, you can be the one to change the conversation and not just sit silently hoping for things to shift.

We've learned who we are in Christ and that our identity needs to be formed and established in Him. We've seen the real battle at hand that we are not waging war against one another, but against the flesh, the spiritual principalities of darkness, and the enemy roaming around looking to devour believers and take them out. We know that God uses His Church and the love believers have for one another to reach the lost. We have identity, we are aware, and we have purpose.

Knowing these things, we can remain eager and hopeful, maintaining unity in our local churches. Not thinking something is too small to become a wedge which can slowly separate what was meant for unity. There have been many times when I said something with good intentions or not really thinking, and it hurt someone. I've tried not to overlook those moments but to make sure if it is at all possible on my part to maintain peace with the people in my life.

I have driven many times over the years, late at night, to a family or friend's house to pursue peace, to ask for forgiveness, to plead my heart and intention, knowing how the enemy would love to devour what was and could be as we grow in unity. I challenge you to be a forgiver. Let it be the thing you are known for. Quick to forgive, quick to restore. The Word says let those who are spiritual restore.

I want to be a restorer, in fact, I want our local churches to be full of restorers instead of offense.

As we near the end of this week, let us remember that our families, friends, churches, and communities need believers who choose to be present, not distracted. They need us to look and listen with intention, to be slow to speak and quick to pray and believe the best. To gather on purpose, not forsaking what's been entrusted, souls all around us. The Lord wants to use us to extend His reach together, through His Body. Let us prefer and honor one another well—supporting and caring for the women in our lives, homes, and communities. Extending forgiveness and keeping our hearts pure. Whether they have just been born or are aging, let us be available to God for them. To continue gathering, seeing, noticing, caring, and pursuing peace at all costs.

My prayer for you is this: **may you remain faithful to God and His redemptive plan in spite of the world, in spite of the fear or pain, in spite of anything that would hinder you or the unity of the church.** I believe you are here to heal, seeking clarity, and pursuing your purpose. Here we are, Lord, send us into your field to reap the harvest of your beloved souls. We are here to gather, to build your presence in our communities. Here we are, proud to be Local Church Girls— send us.

TIME TO REFLECT AND REJECT

What did God reveal to you in this chapter?

_____

_____

_____

_____

_____

_____

Is there something that you need to release so that your arms are available to gather God's precious people?

_____

_____

_____

_____

_____

_____

Have you run your race, weighed down, growing weary along the way?

_____

_____

_____

_____

_____

_____

Have you spent time trying to replicate someone else's needs in your own life based on their success? If so, how can you be more intentional in seeking God for your specific needs in Christ?

_____

_____

_____

_____

_____

_____

How can you begin to gather others into His house? Ask the Lord to open your eyes to see who is right in front of you.

_____

_____

_____

_____

_____

_____

Have you found yourself competing or comparing yourself to others? If so, what is one thing you can do to honor or celebrate someone else's win?

_____

_____

_____

_____

_____

_____

Remember God's character is to leave the 99 for the 1, may it be ours too.

PLANTED OR POTTED
WEEK 6

PLANTED OR POTTED
Week 6

Where you are planted will either reveal your full potential or trap and bind it.

Rooted in Christ, Planted in Purpose. The Local Church Girl is proud to be planted in the House of God, unoffended, healed, redeemed, restored, and anointed to be His hands and feet in her world.

What if the story I shared with you at the very beginning about my friend not being planted in a local church because of something hindering her, and the other precious women in my life experiencing some hesitation or resistance, weren't the norm anymore? What if all the women we knew who were saved were no longer hindered, but instead deeply planted in their local church communities, flourishing and bearing fruit despite anything that might hinder them or their local church? Not only in spite of those things, but also aware now and able to build well and tend wisely with intention and purpose, recognizing the real enemy at hand, not their sister or brother. I write this with a huge smile on my face because it is something I see vividly. I see my sweet friends and family planted in good ground where others are planted beside them. Where the love, support, and transformation they receive flow into their lives, homes, and communities.

My husband and I taught on being fully planted in the ground of your marriage vs staying potted, above the soil. Some of the reasons we stay potted are because of past hurts, fear, and insecurity. Past hurt from other relationships that we still carry wounds from or have built walls to protect us. Fear of not knowing what is going to happen, again related to things that have happened that keep us bound in pots to the what-ifs. Insecurity of our value, worth, or importance. These are the same things that limit us from getting out of our pot and being fully planted within our local churches. We can allow the fears to keep us trapped in a pot where we risk spiritual things like root rot, rootbound, stunted growth, limited fruit-bearing, and church-hopping from place to place, never dealing with why we are still in a pot and how the pot, though it feels safe, is actually hurting us in the long run.

Root rot is when a plant is in a pot that lacks good drainage, leading to the roots suffocating and deteriorating over time. Rootbound is when the plant has been in a pot too long, and its roots get tangled because they are trapped wanting to grow with nowhere to go. Stunted growth occurs when a plant is trying to establish itself in a pot, so it redirects energy from flowering and fruiting to developing its root system within the pot's limitations. This stunting can significantly delay fruit production. Plants need aerated soil because it provides healthy oxygen, room for nutrient absorption, water drainage, and space to establish a strong root system.

With God's help, we can choose to be planted in the mission, vision, and community of our local churches, bearing generous amounts of fruit together and creating a canopy of hope, peace, and blessing. This good ground represents freedom in Christ, and it's full of everything we need to reach our full potential. The examples listed above are just a few of the things that can happen when a plant's potential is trapped or bound to a pot. I would encourage you to pray and ask God how you may still be bound to a pot.

Though we are not bound together through vows like marriage, we are bound together through the Spirit of God to form His body, the Church. This bond is sealed by the Spirit and not words or rings. It is not a covenant cut by people but by God, and He invites us into His faithful covenant of promise and freedom to be sons and daughters, heirs together in Christ.

There are many ways to grow a plant, but placement dictates the growth it is bound to or loosed from. Each plant is given a measure and stature, but what if the measure and stature exceed that of its placement? Then that plant will forever be limited, no matter the measure and stature it was originally given.

Can you see our relation to this? We are each given a measure and stature in life: our original design by God. He intentionally formed each one of us, not missing a detail, even so numbering each hair. But in this world, we are subject to its culture or familial patterns that are replicated, both from sin. These things limit and manipulate our original design because of the fallen state of the world.

But God— I love a good "but God." But God, in His compassion, mercy, and love for us, sent His only begotten Son into the world to save it, not to condemn it. God's redemption plan was and is to restore the whole of creation back to Himself from the powers of darkness and the devil. In Christ, we find our original design. In Christ, we are able to walk out who we are, not a limitation or manipulation of who we are, but the true us, only found in the redeemer Jesus Christ.

I also want to talk to you about the soil which we are cultivators of. By that, I mean we cultivate the ground, creating either a healthy and rich environment for growth, which is not limited, or we don't cultivate the ground. If we don't tend to this responsibility as believers, then our soil is hard because it has never been tilled. The ground is filled with disease and weeds, and it lacks proper hydration and nourishment— not a place you want to be planted.

God teaches us so many biblical truths through His creation. Will we slow down to notice them and activate them in our lives and churches? We need to care for the grounds of our churches. This responsibility should not only fall on the Pastors but should flow down into the congregation so that everyone is a cultivator. The fruit of the Spirit helps us cultivate the soil in our hearts and our local churches. Just as a field needs to be tended to keep the ground healthy, so do our hearts. Look at the amazing qualities of the fruit of the Spirit and think about how they could help you cultivate your own heart towards others and keep the church a place of good ground for all believers.

'But the fruit of the Spirit is love, joy, peace, patience, kindness, goodness, faithfulness,' Galatians 5:22

All of these help keep our hearts and the church's ground good. A place where we grow in the things of God and a place where our heart draws closer to God, reaching others effectively and bearing good fruit. We are nearing the end of this study, and numerous things are at work to undermine believers and the church, aiming to limit or stop the unity we share in Christ through the Spirit. The sinful nature we all have and the principalities of darkness sowing discord, placing wedges, and spreading lies. Our flesh wants to glorify the gifts, placing a higher value on them, lacking love, and literally devaluing the very people we are called to love and grow in the things of God with. I believe that today you are more aware and equipped for the devil's schemes and our flesh's limitations. I'm not telling you to minimize hypocrisy, church hurt, and spiritual abuse. Those things are wrong and ungodly, but I am showing you how to overcome those very real things and not let the enemy use them to trap you and keep you out of church forever.

Sadly, there are some broken and spiritually manipulative or abusive church leaders, but the truth is the media has made it seem as though most churches are like that, when the reality is that most churches are full of really great, honorable leaders and have good ground that you want to be planted in. Good churches that are impacting communities, changing lives, and helping believers cultivate lives of discipleship. Good churches that you can see tangible, fresh fruit from. So don't give up. Don't throw in the towel and say you can't trust people or the church anymore. Learn to walk with a lens of grace and forgiveness. Learn to be sober-minded. Realize who your real enemy is and that it's not God's people or His precious body. You belong in the house of God, whether you've just been saved and your transformation has just begun, or you walked away from the Lord for a while but have come home. No judgment, just restoration in love.

Some of us don't know what it looks like to be planted in the Local Body. We may believe that simply logging in online to catch a sermon and giving is being planted or going to service, only to rush out the door before anyone can get the chance to talk with you.

What about serving as a way of silently being protected by the task, so you're limited from connection and being vulnerable for fear of connection. Those are real examples, and they can blind us from being truly planted. In each of those, the person is bound to a pot by fear. I hope you have been able to locate yourself through this study. Are you a Christmas-and-Easter-only believer (aka a CEO)? Are you too busy to get planted? Have you misunderstood the role of the church in believers' lives? Were you dependent on a leader or someone else's closeness to God rather than God? Have you been spiritually abused by a leader or believer? I'm deeply sorry if it was that last one, as some of my precious family and friends have been on the other side of ungodly leadership. So, what does your pot look like, and how will you take the step to get out of it? Do you need to go to God for healing? Do you need to let go of the past so you can embrace the future? Maybe you've been bound to your pot for so long that you've developed rootbound, and you need help breaking the pot away and careful planting. Whatever your pot and roots may look like, the local church is here to help by the grace and goodness of God.

It will look a little different for each one of us to be planted well in a local body. Some people have the call of the fivefold ministry on their lives (apostle, prophet, evangelist, shepherd/pastor and teacher), so they will naturally look planted in the local body. Others will operate in gifts of the Spirit as the Spirit wills. Some are doctors and pastors— bi-vocational; some are teachers who serve on the greeting team, or faithful evangelists finding people to bring to church. Others are postal workers taking care of the children's check-in cart on Sundays before service, and some are praying mighty prayers behind closed doors and in hospitals and prisons. Being planted is having purpose in the body; it's being used in your unique giftings to bear godly fruit and stir others in the things of Christ. We can all live a testimony before others, and it does not have to be wild and crazy like some think. The power of salvation, no matter what the story, is simply this: **I was lost, but now I am found.**

For the local body of Christ to radiate the glory of God, every joint must supply. Not just teachers, helpers, and admins, but each part seen and unseen. Generosity, encouragement, prayer, administration, evangelism, worship, hospitality, and help, among several other gifts. The local body of Christ reflects the goodness and character of God that frees people from the real replication and bondage of sin. In Christ, there is healing and restoration for people, marriages, and families. There is comfort for the grieving and a family for the lonely. There is hope for the hopeless and strength for the weary. There is a true purpose for the one seeking meaning. God's church is the most powerful place to be planted, and we should be proud to be part of it and create an environment people desire to be in.

God commands a blessing on unity, and if we can grab hold of that truth and promise together, then the church will explode. We will see the multitudes run to the Savior of the world.

Behold, how good and pleasant it is when brothers dwell in unity!
Psalm 133:1

'I therefore, a prisoner for the Lord, urge you to walk in a manner worthy of the calling to which you have been called, with all humility and gentleness, with patience, bearing with one another in love, eager to maintain the unity of the Spirit in the bond of peace. '
Ephesians 4:1-3

Finally, all of you, have unity of mind, sympathy, brotherly love, a tender heart, and a humble mind.
1 Peter 3:8

I appeal to you, brothers, by the name of our Lord Jesus Christ, that all of you agree, and that there be no divisions among you, but that you be united in the same mind and the same judgment.
1 Corinthians 1:10

I will end with one of my favorite passages of Scripture found in John 17, just before Jesus is arrested. It gives us a glimpse of heaven and true unity. Not only that, but this is the longest recorded prayer of Jesus that He prayed for himself, His disciples, as well as you and me. This passage shows Jesus as our forever High Priest and His deep desire that His body—the church—believers— would be one and glorify God in their unity. Let this passage captivate your heart and reveal the grand magnitude of unity in powerful, holy words still as true today as the day Jesus spoke them.

This is called **"The High Priestly Prayer"**

'When Jesus had spoken these words, he lifted up his eyes to heaven, and said, "Father, the hour has come; glorify your Son that the Son may glorify you, since you have given him authority over all flesh, to give eternal life to all whom you have given him. And this is eternal life, that they know you, the only true God, and Jesus Christ whom you have sent. I glorified you on earth, having accomplished the work that you gave me to do. And now, Father, glorify me in your own presence with the glory that I had with you before the world existed. "I have manifested your name to the people whom you gave me out of the world. Yours they were, and you gave them to me, and they have kept your word. Now they know that everything that you have given me is from you. For I have given them the words that you gave me, and they have received them and have come to know in truth that I came from you; and they have believed that you sent me. I am praying for them. I am not praying for the world but for those whom you have given me, for they are yours. All mine are yours, and yours are mine, and I am glorified in them. And I am no longer in the world, but they are in the world, and I am coming to you. Holy Father, keep them in your name, which you have given me, that they may be one, even as we are one. While I was with them, I kept them in your name, which you have given me. I have guarded them, and not one of them has been lost except the Son of destruction, that the Scripture might be fulfilled. But now I am coming to you, and these things I speak in the world, that they may have my joy fulfilled in themselves. I have given them your word, and the world has hated them because they are not of the world, just as I am not of the world. I do not ask that you take them out of the world, but that you keep them from the evil one. They are not of the world, just as I am not of the world. Sanctify them in the truth; your word is truth. As you sent me into the world, so I have sent them into the world. And for their sake I consecrate myself, that they also may be sanctified in truth. "I do not ask for these only, but also for those who will believe in me through their word, that they may all be one, just as you, Father, are in me, and I in you, that they also may be in us, so that the world may believe that you have sent me. The glory that you have given me I have given to them, that they may be one even as we are one, I in them and you in me, that they may become perfectly one, so that the world may know that you sent me and loved them even as you loved me. Father, I desire that they also, whom you have given me, may be with me where I am, to see my glory that you have given me because you loved me before the foundation of the world. O righteous Father, even though the world does not know you, I know you, and these know that you have sent me. I made known to them your name, and I will continue to make it known, that the love with which you have loved me may be in them, and I in them."'

I don't know if you have ever read this passage of Scripture, but the more I read it, the more my heart yearns for this to be so here on earth as it was and is in heaven, radiating in our churches around the globe. I'm so thankful for you, sweet friend, for picking up this book and getting this far. It shows that you are looking for hope and believe in the church, or you are curious and want to cultivate a healthy atmosphere in your local body. I have prayed for you and thank God for you. I pray these words, and the words of the Holy Spirit will permeate your heart and soul, to reveal, heal, release and strengthen you. There is so much work to do. Not alone but together, where every joint supplies, lacking no good thing and limited by nothing.

'How wonderful, how beautiful, when brothers and sisters get along! It's like costly anointing oil flowing down head and beard, flowing down Aaron's beard, flowing down the collar of his priestly robes. It's like the dew on Mount Hermon flowing down the slopes of Zion. Yes, that's where God commands the blessing, ordains eternal life.'
Psalms 133:1-3 MSG

TIME TO REFLECT AND REJECT

So, where are you planted, or are you still in a pot? What do you think is causing hesitation or limiting you in fear? Unpack this with the Holy Spirit.

_____

_____

_____

_____

_____

What are the areas the Lord has opened your eyes to in this study?

_____

_____

_____

_____

_____

_____

How can you begin to cultivate the ground of your heart and your local church?

_____

_____

_____

_____

_____

_____

Call to action: How will you live, serve, and love differently now?

_____

_____

_____

_____

_____

Do you need to pursue peace with someone?

_____

_____

_____

_____

_____

Do you need to put yourself out there and serve in a ministry or even join a small group?

_____

_____

_____

_____

_____

_____

Do you have untapped spiritual gifts you have been sitting on for fear of failure or limitation?

_____

_____

_____

_____

_____

_____

Almost done...

AFTER THE STUDY
EXTRAS

BUSTING MYTHS

I hope that, as you've read this study, God has helped you bust some myths or false beliefs along the way. We want to be as wise as the devil, who is our real enemy. He is the father of lies since the beginning, manipulating truth to turn humanity against God and keep us from the unity God has for us as believers.

Let's examine a few more lies and manipulations of truth that only cause people to resist God and the local body, hindering its full potential when every person fulfills their place in the body. It's important to be aware of these so that we don't fall into them and we can help others see the truth and live in the grace of Christ. Manipulations and lies distort God's grace and redemptive plan, leaving people in bondage. I've started with the myth but replaced it with the truth to help you overcome.

Myths vs Truth

Myth: If I start going to church, they are going to make or expect me to go to everything and start serving every Sunday.
Truth: If you start going to church the transforming love of God will compel you to want to connect in ministries that relate to you and as you grow you will want to serve others and help them find the same joy you have found being planted in your local

church. If someone starts making you feel like you have to serve, shames you, or expects you to serve and go to everything, it's a them issue, don't label the whole church because a couple of people are still growing.

Myth: The Church will only use me for what I can offer. They don't really care about me.

Truth: There is a big difference between being used by God and being used by people. God uses the unique giftings and differences of His people to build and strengthen His Church for His glory. In a healthy church, leadership genuinely cares for you, not just what you can do. Many churches have things like Growth Track, Membership, or DNA Classes to create a safe covering for people who are planted in that Church. The covering is not about control but about protection, development, and direction. Just as pastors have a covering through their ordination for accountability and to ensure their well-being, believers should also have a similar support system. Look at how God models this himself. God is the head of Jesus, Jesus is the head of the Church, the husband is the head of the wife, and parents are the head of the children. God clearly uses the covering for care, accountability, and unity. When we are planted within God's covering, we flourish and are cared for.

Myth: I will have no life if I start going to church. I'll be bored.

Truth: You will have a life full of purpose and deep meaning and will absolutely not be boring. Miracles, testimony, life change, joy, and contentment are not boring.

Myth: Church is for people who really need it. I'm already a good person.

Truth: Our idea of a "good person" is a manipulation of the truth. We have all sinned and fallen short of perfection, beginning with Adam when he sinned against God; sin is in us now. Just because we don't deal with a sin that outwardly looks worse than others do not negate the fact that sin is sin. So, whether you killed someone or stole something, one offense makes you a sinner. Only God is good, and only Jesus, who never sinned though being tempted in all ways, could die for our redemption, restoring us to the Father, not our actions or idea of being a "good person". We all need God and the church.

Myth: You can't trust the church leaders or Pastors.

Truth: Sadly, there have been pastors and Christian leaders who have failed and caused deep hurt. If that has been your experience, I am truly sorry. No one should be wounded by those entrusted to shepherd God's people. My prayer is that you would find healing in Jesus and hope for future relationships with pastors and leaders who reflect His heart.

The truth is, many pastors and church leaders serve with integrity, love, and humility. God calls them to a higher standard of accountability because of the responsibility placed on them. Please don't let the failures of some or even headlines magnify people's weaknesses and keep you from experiencing the blessing of godly leadership in your life.

Myth: I don't have the time to go to Church.
Truth: You don't have time for things that are not important to you, but when they become important and have value, you make the time. Being planted in the Local Body does not mean you are overwhelmed by commitment; your Pastor or leaders should help you find a healthy balance and rhythm for your church life. Being planted looks a little different for everyone. Just because Suzy Sunday is working full-time and serving full-time does not mean that you have to do everything she is.

Myth: I'm too far gone; I can't be forgiven or even redeemed, I belong in hell.
Truth: We all belong in hell. My husband said this once, "If you are looking for fair, look no further, hell is fair. Heaven, however, is the most unfair place in all of creation." There is nothing you can do to receive the gift of grace freely given to us by God through His perfect Son, Jesus, who died for all our sins and restores us completely to the Father if we only believe in Him. So, no dear friend, you are not too far gone. The moment you ask for

forgiveness and recognize that God sent His only Son, Jesus, to die for our penalty of sin is the moment you are saved and redeemed.

Myth: People will judge me, and I don't fit in.
Truth: Some people might judge you, but again, that is a them issue, not a you issue. Just because a couple of people judge and label us does not mean we will never find a good church. Don't give up, keep trying, and soon you will find a good church to be planted in.

Myth: I need to be better before I go.
Truth: Jesus says, "Come", come to find peace and eternal life. There's no need to try to clean up before you run to Jesus; only His perfect sacrifice can cleanse you. No matter how hard you try without Him to be pleasing or good enough for God, you cannot. We need the new life He gives when people receive Christ as their Lord and Savior. The church is full of broken people who are being transformed together. It's okay to come to Jesus in your current state.

There are more myths that keep us from being fully planted and make the church look like an unsafe or unimportant place. Just remember, no church is perfect because it is filled with people who are still being sanctified and saved. Church is not a place of perfection it is a place of freedom, truth and community with others growing in the things of God.

What is your view of the local church? **Is it now the hope of the world with a resounding yes! To go therefore and make disciples baptizing them in the name of the Father, Son and Holy Spirit?** Will you rise up and champion others and protect the house of God. Will you step into the healing you need to get out of your pot and into good ground? You can do all things through Christ who strengthens you. Don't pick up the weight and fear of the what if's, just trust God one step at a time, day by day, little by little.

'May our sons in their youth be like plants full grown, our daughters like corner pillars cut for the structure of a palace; ' Psalm 144:12

' "And it shall come to pass afterward, that I will pour out my Spirit on all flesh; your sons and your daughters shall prophesy, your old men shall dream dreams, and your young men shall see visions. Even on the male and female servants in those days I will pour out my Spirit. "And I will show wonders in the heavens and on the earth, blood and fire and columns of smoke. The sun shall be turned to darkness, and the moon to blood, before the great and awesome day of the Lord comes. And it shall come to pass that everyone who calls on the name of the Lord shall be saved. For in Mount Zion and in Jerusalem there shall be those who escape, as the Lord has said, and among the survivors shall be those whom the Lord calls.'

Joel 2:28-32

The Spirit of God has been poured out on all flesh. How will you step into all that God has entrusted to you?

_____

_____

_____

_____

Before we end this study, I wanted to fill you with hope and encouragement with a little list of some benefits of being planted in the local church:

- Find community, a place of unity and growth.
- Support for hardship, struggle, or pain.
- Accountability to grow and mature in Christ.
- Love, not condemnation or criticism.
- Genuine, selfless friendships.
- Gain wisdom from learning and talking about God's Word together.

- Celebrate transformation; together, you see how God changes lives.
- Family in Christ—you have a deep sense of belonging.
- Missional purpose together for the heart and purpose of your church.
- Community impact influenced by the unity of love and oneness within your church body.
- Freedom from bondage.
- Miracles only God can do.

And the list goes on... Our journey in Christ is also an adventure of faith, and our faith is safe in Christ. I sincerely encourage you to find a local body and get planted. Take your time but also don't look for perfection. Allow the Holy Spirit to guide you to a faithful house, and watch your life be blessed by the community of God.

For the one who longs

What about this very real scenario. Some people do not have access to a thriving Christian Church full of the teachings of the entire bible. Instead, they find a religious institution, and when guests enter, the disconnect is strong. Reading from only the Old Testament, even in old Latin, all the way to neglecting things like healing and the role of the Holy Spirit in believers' lives. The messages are unrelatable, and there is no expounding on the Word of God to teach the believer deeper things. Dry readings and ceremonial repetitiveness make the church feel more like a task than a living relationship that believers are yearning to grow in together. Christmas tends to be the only highlight of the year because people get to sing along to songs they know, surrounded by beautiful Christmas decor and lights; for once, the church feels alive. I've even seen how giving in religious places has nothing to do with the heart of giving, just a passing of a plate or bucket with no meaning or purpose, overlooking and misunderstanding what it is to be a cheerful giver and trust God not our own efforts and funds, while literally getting to be the hands and feet that fund the effective reach of a local church in their community with no lack just people who's treasure is souls.

If you have found yourself in this place, do not be discouraged. Just as it can take some time to find the right doctor or counselor you feel comfortable communicating with, it can also take time to find the right place to plant yourself. It's tempting to stop after a couple of discouraging experiences and decide that church will never work for you, or you will never find your home. But I would plead with you not to grow weary and to count on God's help to lead you to the right place with the right people.

I feel deeply for areas that are limited in churches and pastors filled with grace and God's love. I would even go as far as to challenge you to find opportunities to fund church plant ministries locally and globally. If everyone in Palm Beach County were to try to attend church, there would not be enough churches, let alone enough pastors to care for and help grow the precious and beloved people.

Think about the global lack. Even events like the COVID-19 pandemic have changed the way people connect with their local church. And some people who faithfully watched the online services to stay connected during the pandemic have grown comfortable attending at a distance, missing the blessing of being known and building community in person.

There is something powerful about our senses in the natural that are not distorted or even disconnected through digital platforms that helps us care, support, and love each other even better. Even Paul desired to encourage people face-to-face, longing to be with them because he knew his letters, though powerful and from God, lacked the benefit of being together. Technology cannot replace in-person gatherings. There are numerous challenges that continue to face the local church, such as the high cost of living and operational expenses. And yet that is no surprise to God. He calls believers to support His church, each other and not neglect gathering.

There are many precious people who have grown up in environments like the one above or even those who have experienced it for a moment, only to want nothing to do with it. Like we saw earlier in this study, the body of Christ is a powerful and life-giving place for the individual and the community at large. My heart is to help reclaim the value and importance of the local churches around the globe, and that more and more girls would be proud to be Local Church Girls, planted and expanding God's goodness together. I believe the Local Church Girl notices the souls on the fringe. People who have been hurt, believed a myth or lacked a good place to plant themselves. We need to pray for the local body at large. That God would pour out blessings and provision to fund the local churches and people who step out in faith to answer the call of the five-fold ministry. We are here for closeness, not competition, closeness through connection and community all in the name of Christ.

There are other myths or misinterpretations of the church that keep us from being fully planted and make the church look like an unsafe or unimportant place. Just remember, no church is perfect because it is filled with people who are still being sanctified and saved. Church is not a place of perfection it's a place of freedom, truth and community with others growing in the things of God through the power of Jesus transforming lives.

Striving is not from God, but a healthy rhythm is, and Jesus modeled that in His life. Being planted looks different for the worship leader and the prayer warrior. It looks different for the event decorator and the nursery helper. It looks different for a life group leader and someone who is joining a life group.

We can't compare ourselves to others in the church; otherwise, we will do things outside of grace and under pressure. We are here for closeness. We are not meant to compete with each other as the enemy, and our flesh want. Overvaluing and labeling others, creating clicks, and making people earn righteousness.

Like Paul shared in Ephesians chapter 4, together the church builds itself up in love. So, remember and get this deep in your heart, "The local church is still God's plan — and you are part of it." Let's do all that we do in love.

Tips For Being Planted

For New Believers:

- Find a local church. I recommend an ARC Church or Rhema Bible Collage Church; both are Spirit filled ministries and provide a covering for the church associated with them.

- Show up regularly. The more you lean into the body of Christ, the more you are blessed by its benefits. There is a "great grace" that covers the body of Christ that is different from the grace we receive individually from Christ. *See Acts 4.*

- Stay planted in the house of the Lord with other believers until Jesus comes back to receives His bride.

For Seasoned Believers (Who may have experienced hurt or being disconnected.)

- Know why you are in a pot?
- Seek peace with other believers and extend forgiveness.
- If peace is found, stay, believe the best, and keep pursuing peace.

- If peace cannot be made, don't give up.
- Eat and take a nap, recover and get back out there, Find another church.
- Leave your past experience of hurt behind. Do not bring it into any church you are looking to be planted in.
- Don't ignore red flags, but remember no church is perfect because all of us are still being sanctified.
- Get out of your pot and live with the lens of grace.
- Bear fruit
- And dwell in the house of the Lord with other believers till Jesus comes back to receives His bride.

Time To Invite

The goal of this study was to help you see the body of Christ/The Church the way God intends it to be, as well as your part in it. Now that you've completed this six-week study, it's time to prayerfully seek the Lord on who to invite to church and how. Remember not to pick up the pressure if you feel the nudging of the Holy Spirit. If God asks you to invite someone or even share Jesus with them, that means He has prepared their heart. All you have to do is walk in obedience, no pressure, literally. It might be hard the first couple of times, but the more you do it, the more you will see God's got you.

Here are some creative, thoughtful, and loving ways to invite someone to church with you.

- Offer them a ride and get their favorite drink so they can enjoy it on the ride.
- Ask them to sit with you and make a point to meet them in the parking lot or entrance, so they don't feel like they have to go searching for you in a place they have never been.
- Uber them
- Take them out to lunch after and pay for them.
- Offer to help with household duties after church so they can hear the good news and hopefully gain a church family.

- Send them a pic of you sitting next to an empty seat saying, "Wish you were here, join me next week!"
- Buy them a bible and put a handwritten note inside inviting them to church on a specific date.

Sample Text Message:

Hey sweet friend, I'm going to church this Sunday and would love to invite you to come with me. Then we can grab coffee or lunch after, my treat.

For a friend or neighbor who has little kids:
Hey friend, I'd love to invite you and your family to join us at church, and then afterward, we can take our kids to the park for a picnic.

Hey friend, my family and I would be honored to invite you to church with us, and then we can grab ice cream afterward.

There are so many thoughtful ways to invite someone to church. It doesn't have to be weird; it just needs to be intentional. So, pray it through and be proud to ask someone to find hope and community through Jesus and His church.

You're Invited!

TO GET PLANTED IN YOUR LOCAL CHURCH

on ANY DAY
at ANY TIME

1 BODY OF CHRIST ST., WRLD, ANY CITY

You Go Girl!

Cheering you on in Christ!
Nicole

Connect with me online at www.localchurchgirl.com or follow me on Instagram at @localchurchgirl_ & @nicoledebehnke

Made in the USA
Middletown, DE
18 November 2025

20885996R00076